The Ascent Of Monte Grappa

Howard Barker

The Ascent Of Monte Grappa

JOHN CALDER : LONDON
RIVERRUN PRESS : NEW YORK

First published in Great Britain, 1991, by
  John Calder (Publishers) Ltd.,
  9–15 Neal Street, London, WC2H 9TU
and in the United States of America, 1991, by
  Riverrun Press Inc
  1170 Broadway
  New York, NY 10010

British Library Cataloguing in Publication Data
Barker, Howard, 1946–
  The ascent of Monte Grappa.
  I. Title
  821.914
  ISBN 0–7145–4202–4
Library of Congress Cataloging in Publication Data
Barker, Howard.
  The ascent of Monte Grappa / Howard Barker
    p. cm.
  ISBN 0–7145–4202–4 :
  I. Title
    PR6052.A6485A94   1990
  821'9142 — sc 20   90–48103
                                              CIP

Printed in Great Britain by Delta Press, Brighton.
Typeset at Oxford University Computing Service.

To The One
Who Knows Who She Is

Contents

The Ascent of Monte Grappa

In 1901 Pope Pius X ascended Monte Grappa to erect a calvary

In 1917 Grappa was the site of terrible warfare

In 1918 the struggle was repeated

In 1932 it became an Official Military Monument

I

I will scale the Grappa
Said the Pope
This being the mountain of mountains
And plant a cross
For God loves all high places
There specially He dwells

2

Such a torrent of explosive
Fell upon the crest
Night turned to day you could not say
Where one burst ceased
You could not separate the detonations
Or penetrate the curtain of fragmenting
Stone

3

Let the shadow of your hip fall on my eyes
Your nakedness will put horizons to anxiety

Lay your travelled cheek to my intemperance
How much of my invective you endure

Perhaps this time we shall not arrive
At a conclusion
Perhaps this time

4

There was no road to Grappa
This clinging
This tormenting
Doubled like a bowel
Track of impatience
They made for the descent of corpses
Reckless
Chauffeurs
Of the Unknown Dead
Is
It
Not
Boring
The
Routine
Transport
Of the bloodless and the uncomplaining?
The smashed were company
The pulped were musical
On every bend their damaged chorus came!
But these!

He rode side-saddled on a mule
Reticent in white
And when pain came conceded
Relieving himself in the sight
Of porters and chroniclers
His urine sparkling in the sun

A Christ
Recumbent
A Christ
In sections numbered
And a cross in interlocking parts
Ascended in the rear
The joiners also
Not without convictions
And a clerk of the Holy Office
A casual mountaineer

They parted from the sunlight
At twelve thousand feet
And swimming cloud
Experienced the inhibition on
Conviviality that blindness brings

This silence he preferred
Thinking the mountain scorned
Inconsequential things
Only when the guides conferred

Was there some tattle
The forlorn chink of coffee pans
In beading moisture

6

We are rising by the tarmac road
Our car lifts us so easily
Smelling of industry
Its odours of pressed laminates
Its brittle and unpassionate form

Your knee is raised
Your wrist requires so little purchase
On the wheel
While I sit placid as a relic
Borne on its annual tour by priests

Today you are expressing less
Today you move without the restlessness
That marks you in a crowd
Today you imagine without words

This place was once so loud

Stop in this cleft
Here where the road permits
And let the engine die

Grappa the Silent

Your fingers moving to the key
Are insubstantial as a moth
And the stopped wipers pitifully
Pile against the screen

Today you say nothing clever
Or perceptive
Today you have the character of
A room newly vacated
Which bears the marks of absent
Furnishing
Today there is so little of you left

This place was once so populated

From this point we must walk
Keeping a little distance
For our separate thoughts
Your loved clothes are audible to me
Your stockings the colour of smoke
Your coat's bickering seams

Soon we must talk
Soon
Being what we are
We must give this discomfort form

The lips of howitzers were pursed
At forty-five degrees
Like children's for goodnights

In orchards superfluous searchlight teams
Smoked or defecated in the sun

Not one would risk more than
The discipline obliged

At the first crack
They would consign their badges
To the vineyard floor and run

The buttons and the brassards
Of disintegrating dynasties
A scattered blossom of catastrophe

Far from loved cities pining trains
Lay hollow eyed
Their couplings still
The dying crawled beneath them for their shade

And in the brief hiatus
Between one army's passage
And the next
The fountain in the square displayed
A withering political indifference

Perhaps it is time to return to the car?

Rain rinses the rim of an abandoned winch
Whose motor is an orange fossil
Brilliant as a sun
And the mouths of dugouts are
Fresher than cut stems

We are standing in the hush of the obliterated
We who are so excellently bred
How could they fail to admire us?

If they were paraded wouldn't the dead
Like dogs with their muzzles in our palms
Murmur
Like horses with their lips to our hands
Mutter
How fine you late products of calamity are?

Certainly it is time to return to the car

But lend me a conclusion
Or are you overwhelmed?
Discover a perspective
Or are you ashamed of this undamaged life?

Affirm the meaning of pain
The inevitable nature of pain
Its significance
Its recurrence
Shh
Beloved

We must live in the ashes of the extinguished
We must walk in all broken places uncurtailed

9

His mundane prayer dismissed them to their tents
He could not be spontaneous
He never could invent nor fake a fluency
Speech was a broken pavement which he
Scrutinized for faults
A senile walker china boned

Yet in the council he had shown dexterity
Drawing doctrinal conflicts to a close
With a form of words
He was the single candidate the majority
Agreed not to oppose
And these God also loves
The dry-handed and impeccable
These might also know His preference

His God was barrel-chested
His God moved stones

A God of labour who in all weathers
Filled with such practised movements
The holes in Trentine roads

A solitary with whom he had long
Ceased to speak

A crouching form seen under trees
Never employing more than a necessary strength

In the quick drop of darkness
This Pope lay still and hardly warm
He heard his clerk move water in a canvas bowl
Then toss it out
He listened to the scoured throats of men
The practised steps of privacy in confined space
And felt the mountain move between them

Lifting his head
He strained for the hum of its bulk

He trawled silence
As we hang horror on the single footfall
Inexplicable in the night

And it was silent
It hid from him

Neither indicating God
Nor His necessity

Grappa wears its cemetery
As patient animals submit to infant blows

Landscape knows
The passing nature of human offence
The little damage pride or pity might do

SOLDIERS OF THE GRAPPA
GLORY
TO
YOU

WE WHO COME AFTER
HAIL
YOUR
SACRIFICE

The Latin numerals bestow propriety
On disfigurement
And these pavilions with no populace
Command a sense of absence yet

Not of a Roman permanence
The paving cracks beneath the ice
And winters wear out platitudes

Loved one
Explain the poorness of a life
And by what right we measure
Explain the power of circumstance
And its limited command

Loved one
You so widely read
And the daughter of Christians
Testify
To freedom's endless making
Or the blindness of all choice

We casually among these bones
We circumspect among them
Are living the requirement of a time
No less than these shelved fragments
Sealed only for the hour of neglect

Even our first encounter was unchosen
And our parting will have merely
The appearance of consideration
The weighing of advantages
In palms rubbed smooth from passionate strife

The summit he approached alone
An envoy from the city wrapped in wind

How undespotic he appeared inverted in the lens
A motion of such solitude
As aged parents make who for the last time part
From children long grown out of need

The camera staggered after him unwieldy as a gun

Boxes clattered
And fumbled negatives clanged in the breech
Had there before been anyone so hung
Between humility and art?

He acted faith for faith's sake
In a time obsessively mechanical

He simulated his devotions
In a time incorrigibly systematical

He ached for the light to be right
While men in libraries inscribed
Iron laws of social motion
And painters in cool halls
Idolized machines

Christ knocked together
Rose to a polite applause

All Lombardy was underneath His feet
A tray of cities
While the mountain man-blind
And love-ignorant
Gave neither pope nor porter cause
To doubt this calvary's permanence

13

Body of patience belly-marked from births
Glazed in evaporations of erotic prayer
And finished with a hundred hands
Room-washed
Oath-tinted
The itinerary of infatuations
Inked along your thighs

March by me

I applaud your labours
Relentless and unexpired mouth
I watch with the critical and practised eye
Of your historian
The angle of your hip
The subtle extrusion of the lip
In male company

15

March by me

Even the doorman knows your policy
And drawing through the chains
Hangs his last look on your departing walk

How quiet the Grappa is tonight
And I potential memory
How it crouches
And I inevitable passage
Let us be sparing in our talk

In this wet shadowed square of gravel
Down these steep-angled flights of
Restless lantern light
We move with the impeccable deportment
Of a mature love
A statesman of a petty principality
A woman too frequently betrothed

We keep our declarations to a minimum
Having learned to postpone
We forgo expression of the obvious
Having disowned all sentiments
Of implacable fidelity

We have made the ascent and descent
We have stood on the peak breathless with
Incredulity

And now must learn to love the low
Perhaps the time has come
Perhaps

To substitute for hunger calculation
Making texts of absences
And rituals of dissimulation

Failing together all tests of excellence
We might succeed in keeping the uncertain
A
  Need
      Denied
         Decay

14

God wanted
God certainly did not impede the will of those who
Wanted
God wanted therefore

God pitied
God certainly did not disguise the pain of those who
Suffered
God pitied therefore

The worldwide dying of an unlucky class
Whose graves sand or snow smothered
Possess the comic character of historic wars
Whose relics blurred by dust or verdigris
Are the inert stuff of the museum

Fortunate the far-dispersed limbs of the exploded man
Whose fragments sailed beyond
The scope of diligent discovery

In some crow crevice the bone might hiss
Outside the beckoning of politics

I am not substance for your piety
Nor pretext for your mutiny

But one who was born in an avalanche of time

15

Mountain
Impeccable encounters leave you cold
The exertions of believers
The panic of the unconvinced

Mountain
My own silence might darken even yours

I shall be granite to all theorists
And their regiments

Pontiffs
States
Spurious griefs

I shall borrow your contempt for laws

But
Mountain
You are too ironic

I'll be a chemist of unstable elements
Combining little acts of conscience
With plotted pleasure

Observing
Days lost to irresolution
Debts owed to the coercive
And the dispersal of the intellect's
Accumulated treasure

But
Mountain
I must not know all

When Christ flew into fragments
One man of multiple delusions
Climbed from the trench relic-obsessed

His crawl
Absurd
His wriggle
Fatuous
Big arsed peasant worming
On the white scar of the crest
Whose blessed idiocy
Mocked comprehensiveness

On Being a Despot's Foot Stool

How hard to assert the philosophical when you are on
                                                    your knees
How difficult to retrieve the compensations

All these I have rehearsed

> *Time's mockery of potentates*
> *The knife behind the courtier's smile*
> *The comedy of disease*

But with my forehead to the stirrup
The crushed pulp of my pride drips out my eyes
Enhancing his satisfaction

How difficult to see the humour in our altered states
                                        when you are trod
Or the possibilities hid in catastrophe

All these I have identified

> *New sympathy with the abject*
> *Vanity's extinction*
> *Nearness to a suffering God*

But kneeling in the drain
The rotted cloth of my ambition chokes my mouth
He smilingly observes

I wish him dead and all the world's shit
Watered him

I wish his skewered infants waved on
Bamboos

I wish his heart were drawn through his
Ribs

And pumping held for famished dogs to
Fasten on

I wish his bowel were ravelled four times
Round the temple

I wish his eyeballs swung from nerves
Like skipping ropes

I wish his testicles were rolled in
Mills

Oh, and for his tongue!

I wish this prick of malice such an
Infliction of imagination

To make the most clotted and febrile
Torturer shut up shop

No

No

This catalogue relieves me

Don't ask me to stop!

I shall die of humiliation
Which is possible for the proud

Discovered in my pit
With my knees drawn to my mouth

It will rain more heavily than usual
Rats will make off with the fingers

And in a distant city prayers will be uttered
And regiments equipped with light tunics

In which to avenge me

I could not wait
I could not bear to need to wait

I could not bear the thought
Every nerve was not strummed

How corrupt the Romans have become
They squander the taxes
That might have delivered me
On boulevards and elephants

(Valerian, Roman Emperor and Persian foot stool, died in captivity circa 248 AD)

Madman's Jug

When at the slowest pulse of night
Child flung
Mouth hung
And slack bellied
The madman tips his temper out
Permit its flood to shake your tower
It is his tribute to the love-spoiled
And necessary
This defiling of the inert hour

He like some wild pope of insomnia
He like the grinning and so-modern councillor
Discovers dark to be his honest store

You shall never know abandon such as this
Were you abandoned by the single perfect love
Listen therefore

The words go higher than the night plane's flicker
As it carves the cream-black sky to Nova Scotia
The words go higher than the beams of radar men
Working on cold islands their unwarlike shifts
The oaths of neverlove
The repudiation of charity's unwholesome gifts

Listen then
To the mouth which is a jug

Tonight he will paddle the sky with a broom
And his boat will be the broken bath
Of his despotic and unyielding room

Tonight he will at last locate his enemy
For somewhere he exists
The One Responsible
Who banned him from all intimacy
Certainly he exists
And he will stake him by the wrists
To a thin cloud
And watch him perish in the rising sun

*

Piano Concerto No *1*

My train is the plough of undistinguished landscape
Stopping at every signal to divide its day

Was ever a plain so gaoled in resignation or a river
So submissive to the bray
Of an ill-tempered sun?

I could expire in the upholstery
I could be discovered skin and boots
The tape still turning in the brain

Bartok!

I play you to the guilty cranes that stoop
Round-shouldered over docks

I hum you to the arid fields
That are ashamed to bring forth crops

And to the red-haired woman walking with a horse
Down bridleways of dereliction

Dance horse on your forelegs!
Batter your signature with that angelic hoof!
Where are the visionaries of the estuary
Who will ride open-thighed the carriage roof?

I am travelling to love
Or to love's bitter and absurd dissection

I am to sleep in such a narrow bed
Full of the liquor of a night of recollection

And the flying blind of the dawn will show
Low trees groping in sea fog

My train is a marriage that will not die
For fear of silence

My train is a woman who outlives her sons
Tapping a morse on the pavement
For a death that never comes

Climb in and out you bickerers and traders
Extol your legalized misdeeds

Your sandwiches will petrify
Before a mudblack god crawls from the river
And seated in the racks
Plays my master on a pipe of reeds

*

The Character of the Actor

(In memoriam Philip Sayer)

What we ask of the actor is a little thing
That he flings his life's conclusions in the air
And standing like a bride in the falling colours
Weeps with anticipation of inevitable silences

What we require of the actor is a small manoeuvre
That he divides before our very eyes
The common assessments of a drumming world
And proud as the mongrel rebukes even the rain

How still he stands with the unforgivable thought
In his mouth
And a smile as beautiful as the buckled chrome of
Abandoned cars
If there was a regime for his infatuations
Who would not license him?
Irresistible actor
He annihilates shame with his mouth
And his body is a boat for our fugitive claims

*

The English in Lapland

My mistress would sleep with the slit-eyed man
She tells me so

He could lay her out on the cot by the fire
And smelling of fish
Could pulp away the night's thick black
With tales poured down her undefended ear

He could make a child of her again
I almost wish I were not here
But in the city
So that she might say
I lay beneath the hawknosed man
The master and the teller of his race
Still as an infant
In the decorous lamp
And in the morning he gave me permission
To drowse

He sang as he dragged his booming boat
To the sparkling water

Wood smoke
And city labels in my pale blouse

2

The men require me to be weak
I find this simple
Having played impracticality for years

They insist I am bewildered
I find this harder
Having always understood too well

They hurt the table with their fists
And laugh like guns

How riotous they are without their wives

While I only require a bed to dream in

Our eyes meet half-hatefully

It should never came as a surprise
When intellectuals finger knives

3

The Lappish boy
Has recently returned from America
He calls America parochial

The Lappish boy
500 miles from any city
Finds little to admire in the West

Pulling the nets ashore before breakfast
And wielding his knife
As swift as a woman who sews
He expresses the opinion
(Heads in the bucket)
Despite its communications
(Guts in the pail)
And its inordinate resources
(Fins flashing silver still)
In America nobody knows
The sky continues after the horizon

4

The novelist in gutting fish
Has sliced his hand
And wears a rag around
Grinning and ashamed

He feels this reflects on his urban character
He feels these peasants will detect
Some ancient bravery is spoiled

But they are not critical
And in between the heaving of the boat
And the stowing of barrels

Articulate what they find
Unsatisfying in his prose

5

The travelling actors wear with excessive pride
The costume of the country
And beat the instruments with
Too much show
Somehow you know
Real reindeer men don't act their authenticity
The mark of truth is in degeneration

The handsome actor who rubs snow
Against his nakedness
Offers his sex like a bargain
How easy he is to resist

And the grin of the red-cheeked woman
Is a wound in her face
Inflicted by self-consciousness

How jagged their blades of laughter are
As if the softness of the land
Had made marauders of them

6

Night is darkest here
Of all cloaks on the earth the weightiest
To suffocate ambition
And obscure armies

The nationalists are bickering round candles
Listen
Their bottles fall like curses in the grass

Take our towels from the green rail
And holding up the storm lamp
Weave to the ancient sauna
Whose great cold tank booms
Of births and sicknesses

Throw on the tin cup's contents
And see the steam cloud stagger

Open yourself
They guess we are making love
Open yourself
In this dry hush of heat

They are singing songs of their people
Ancient songs about
The power of champions
The fooling of husbands

And the usual reluctance
To serve in the wars

Were you ever more open

The lake is heaving with life

Men Don't Die Like That

The tramp would thrash me with his memory
For showing death like this *
Would lay his scourge of anger down my back

>   Ten for impertinence
>   Ten for irreverence
>   Ten for failing to observe the facts

His medals jangle like drunk girls
His grave mouth gapes for oaths to
Satisfy a violated piety

Suffering lends him authority which he
Transports like an archbishop's hat

He knows
He saw
He yells

Men don't die like that

No use pleading my method
To list theatre's bargains with impossibility
Would be a waste of breath
This high priest of experience can't be gainsaid
He swings his pain over my head

* *Pity in History*, BBC TV, 1985

37

The
    Unrepentant
           Stager
                Of
                    Discord

For I
Though my speculation cruelly offends
Concede nothing to the recollectionist
Knowing fidelity would pulp the heart of art
More savagely than shells did his friends

*

Let Us Marry

What I see in your contemptuous eye
Is my own death

And why not it has to be envisaged

What I see in your lost grace
Is my wilful settling for less

Less always

Weren't you lissome
And now you are merely energetic

Weren't you perceptive
And now you are merely shrewd

What I feel in your tight house
Is poverty's proximity

Its tap on the partitions
Its scuttle in the joists

Didn't I always predict it?

What I find in your body
Is our never discarded infancy

r insincerity
ir incapacity for hiding your ends

n't you know I know your calculations?

Listen
I am a subtle man
None subtler

And your false murmurs
Are if anything more beautiful to me

Than a girl's giving in an afternoon

When I die therefore
Whisper below but loudly

Mutter your temper
Drop crockery
And strike the taps
When putting the kettle on
To whet your lover's dalliance

I should die better then
Delivered of reluctance
And impatient to be gone

Tank Crew

They cramp in the peculiar odour of an innocence
Hanging their limbs on levers

Neither loveless nor perverse they meditate
Among the stencilled numbers

On the quality of bravery its sudden abdication
And the swift arrival of unwelcome choice

To kill might gratify the longing for simplicity
That identifies the military art and yet

They find in one another's eyes no fever of conviction
Only the unpolished gaze of a disabling doubt

The crowd is advancing wielding its weapon Song
And its uplifted shield of pale children

Soon they will blunt the obtuse sides of steel
With warm flesh and drown the barking wireless

With
    Incredulous
        Laughter

*

Timisoara

This gale is the rage of the earth to have been shamed
                                                again
And these torrents are the spilling of maimed clouds
Who limp the land like wounded gods flung out of
                                                heaven
My windows are washed in a frantic rain
My door is gripped in its frame and shaken by the hands
Of the impetuous dead
It was now or never
The half-living said

*

Child
Who
Drowned
In
The
Crowd
Enter my room with your red dresses
The night is flying with the massacred in its arms
Rest
And portray the impatience of those who lifted you
To the many mouths of the encrusted state

*

42

The tanks have brought their silence to the city square
And there is immobility in them such as mourners wear
Who have forfeited every gesture to their grief.

*

The tank which crouches on the snow has the lightness of
                                                a bird
The wind sings melodies between its plates
Inside the uncruel idleness of lives
Susceptible to intimacies and to grace

Their habit is the solitary chance of abject power

*

An Airman in Africa

If it is History when the bookbinder
Wraps up his tools

In cloths oiled against his possible
Return

He was Historical

If it is History when the craftsman
Cleans his bench with such deliberation

And standing finally in the diminished yard
Listens in a novel way
To the murmured registers of infancy and age

He was Historical

Obedient to the summons of the state
He moved on tides of calculations

Smelling dark harbours
While rumour revved his heart

Rehearsing drills
An infinite part
Of military migrations

And drifting from the manifestations of a war
Fetched up an in estuary of unpredicted quiet

A camp in Africa

Here was perfect redundancy to
Exercize imagination in

Here was a gift of plains to call the self
From its impetuous marriages

And rearrange the stacked priorities of
Distant life

A ragged childhood of unwatered streets
And the percussion of slammed doors

The racing river of family
That poverty inflicts on contemplation

The never uncontradicted point of view
He found expired like a death

It was silent
Africa
For all its zoo

Propellors cast their shadows in moonshine
And jackals moved like maids between the huts

While those who had not chosen one another
Lay immobile under nets
Enduring the proximity of self
The unfamiliar climate brings

He paid the debt of laughter to collectivity
Without yielding himself

He studied texts on the behaviour of machinery
And walked long distances by lakes

The world altered

And he
Not unhistorical

Altered also

Musicians, A Café in Strasbourg

They cringe at the door
Appropriately
Artists must move like thieves

They expect to be flung in the road
Correctly
Performers read the signals of impatience

And with practised invisibility
They perch on stools
Reluctant to offend
Even by tuning their instruments

Softly
So as not to bruise a tepid conversation
Rising
From stillness
As a frog drags itself from a pool
Their music rinses the sterile
Laughter from the room

Fiercely they watch their fingers
As if they might escape the wrists
And run along the wires

Infatuated with perfection
They dare their hands with their eyes

They plunge in a sea of brotherhood
Clapping the waves as they rise

Opinion
Dies

I will hold all three in my arms
I will confess the secrets of my will
Until exhausted like a child
Who tells the whole of his plan
I'll sleep stretched over the chairs
Mouth open
And head on my hands

Sleep until
The first knock of the delivery man
Returns my heart
To prejudice and conscience

*

Singer in a Poor School

The girl with the perfect voice sings this love song
Through a fence of coughing
Over a ditch of shifting
Shaping her words like a wet-handed potter
Pulling the lips of a jar

I shall not see you again my fascination

Her coarse face
Her body of beef
Some hook might have deposited on the concert floor
Such bulk of blotched mortality from which
The vowels escape the mouth's unfastened door
And the piano rattles the bones in its jaw

I shall be without my consolation

The sea is foaming on its long runs
The motorcyclist evades death on the bends
How still the moon stands casting on the mattresses
A wealth as false as jagged tin
And the plumber plans the summerhouse
His restless wife will undress for another in

All hours will I seek for thee in vain

They fling their handfuls of applause
They roll their pebbles of politeness down the floor
Warm red she lurches to the clattering canteen
The smacked smile dying down among her peers

How shall I live the loveless years?

Death's Rooms

Light are Death's rooms to the perfectionists
High-ceilinged as old libraries
Where opinion sits in shelves of silent binding

Nothing contradicts

The single chair is still as the spiked insect
Under glass
Neither animation nor emotion
And shadows never pass
As oppression always followed even on the perfect act

No appearance of the poorly loved can spoil the day
And what is placed remains unaltered
Immune to disarray

The floor of honeyed wood is without stains
Of quarrels
And the door is closed against both allies
And antagonists
Neither of whom sustained their pose

No wind in the rafters
No anxious side-stepping of pigeons on the gutter
Only the happy criminality of fairgrounds
Filtered through an opaque glass
Of violet and rose

Bruised Room, Poland

I'd shed particularity
The few hard-hammered points of character
And mineral states of anger from
Which sensibility's refined
Not in order to be nameless
Not to be dissolved in solidarities but
Swimming like a winged seed in draughts
Become so undefined all pains might pass
Simply as blood through the placenta wall
This room is warm as a dropped dress

*

They are not extinguished merely beyond interrogation
The perpetrators breathless and the victims lost to speech
Laughter and disaster can no longer be distinguished
The poverty of judgement slips out of reach
Are they not perfect having no cause to plead?
Are they not kind having nothing to teach?
This room is kind as proffered nakedness

*

On waking the window looks me in the eye
As if all night it had crouched patient as a child
Holding up for my approval its sketch of the sky

*

1989

THE BIRTH OF POLITICS
AND
CULTURAL WARS

My shallow congratulation falls as soot my hollow approval rolls as cans in urban winds this torrent of solidarity from every café in the West will wash away the purity of tempers

IT'S HISTORY BEFORE YOUR VERY EYES
THE BREATHLESS JOURNALISTS DECLARE

The newsmen with their stigmata
The commentators with Historiosis
The writers fixing European seminars

EVERYBODY'S EIN BERLINER, KAMERAD!

THE
MUSEUM
OF THE
PROLETARIAT
IS CLOSED
TODAY

I wanted bells to ring
I ached for bells to ring
Why would the bells not ring
In our cities of

(YOU WILL ALSO HAVE THIS THING)

Our oozing communities of

(YOU WILL ALSO FEEL ITS TONGUE)

Our seeping suburbs of

(A PYTHON ROUND YOUR INNOCENCE)

Entertainment

THE FIRST RESTORATION IS THE TERRIBLE
MODERNITY OF GOD

Amiens to Sofia
Milan to Bucharest
Winchester to Split

```
SOBIESKI
THE
CONDITION OF
VOLTAIRE
1683
```

I summoned bells

BELLS I SAID DON'T WAIT FOR ROPES
But
Split
The
Spoiled
Skies
With
Your
Hammers

Whilst dates are only hooks to swing catastrophes upon
this was a year to carve along the spines of sentimentalists
and determinists both

1989

Europe your smouldering libraries
Europe your cathedrals rising like men from sleep
Their shoulders heaving clouds

AND THE STATUES MUST COME DOWN AGAIN
THE FISTS AND FINGERS
ESPECIALLY THE POINTING FINGERS
MUST COME DOWN AGAIN

Lenin
Stalin
Gottwald

The roar of falling monuments is our culture's music

Their fragments might serve to keep the trolleybus from running down the hill

Please jam the head of the dictator underneath the wheel

(And I had sat my youth in small rooms smoke thick and alcoholic within the peace attentive to the ideologists in English peace perfectly unafraid of the police imagine that fragility ...)

Apollinaire drove in a little car as Europe's lights were flickering on hills

1914

Dogs barked he said as if they knew this evening was the very last

1917

And twice they were required to change the tyre

1919

> ON LITTLE SCREENS AT
> CHRISTMAS POETS STOOD
> WITH COLONELS COAXING
> A NATION OUT OF DEATH
> WHO WILL FORGET THE WAY

They talked at once
They were unskilled at propaganda
They lacked the terrible gift of communication

NO MORE ENGLISH ECONOMISTS IN WARSAW
BY ORDER

They deserve a lovelier gift than these spoiled and rotting
archivists

The Marxist admirers of free markets etcetera

```
         SOBIESKI
           THE
     HERO AND LOVER
           OF
     THINKING WOMEN
          1683
```

(And missing peasants came down from the hills where
they had sheltered from the tracker dogs of the police but
declining to disclose the whereabouts of caves in which)

I also have a cave in roaring England
No I will not tell you where
But later on perhaps we might well share
A candle in its dark

LET US ALL EMBRACE SWIFTLY
EMBRACE AND THEN INVENT A
MIND WITHOUT

UTOPIAS

Nothing was lost
Nothing was extinguished
Neither the sound of anthems nor the flags wrapped in
The bottom of the mind
Nor were all photographs burned in the fires but here an
Uncle
Stands clasping the emblem of an unforgettable regime

TO THE DISMAY OF ENGLISH EDUCATORS THE
TRIBE PERSISTS

Keep quiet about your cave

Look, they are carrying the cabinets of the secret police
to other quarters...

KEEP QUIET ABOUT YOUR CAVE...!

*

Mates of Wrath

Oh
Stop
Staring
Stop
Seeking
Collisions
You thing of the pavements
Did I meet your eyes
Then I apologize

Certainly Christ has been here recently
The houses have the aspect of indifference
That accompanies a prophet's passage
Green railings going brown
The dog with three legs whose collar rings
Certainly He lingered here and lodged
With the woman who fills her windows
With pictures of tortured monkeys

Child crying in the hollow hospital
Ribbon of heart unravelling
I climb on the bins
To catch your disbelief
I dislodge the lids
Which roll away drunk on chloroform

My hairdresser smells cleaner than the clouds
Her eyes are downcast with conspiracy
Look how her shoes like palace guards
Rush her over cracks of hesitation
To her rendezvous with an
Unforgivably
            Innocent
                  Man

The mackerel are churning the water
They thrash the shallows to a batter of scales
I pulled out 87 grins the shopkeeper
We raced along the harbour arm
Clutching our weapons
As befits a massacre

The prostitutes have seized the little window
Their postcards jostle
Their postcards brawl
Their names are black as hairs in the sink
It must be time I visited Jane

In this dusk I'll show your arse
With your permission Madame
To him whose eyes are free

I'll lift your skirt and the
Unoccupied can witness it

The reward of unemployment
A gift to the unscholarly

The shy draper cuts her cloths
And the revolutionist lurches by
How poor his imagination is
He does not give her excellence a glance

How many accommodations he must make
To our fatuous rhythms
His
    face
       explodes
               in
                  yellows
How he must squeeze a succulence
From our false decisions
His
    grin
      is a
          fermenting
                    fruit
He stands aside
While I transport this unwieldy passion
Through streets narrower than mischief

My neighbour came from Lithuania
His large head full of wars and manners
Yesterday he struck a thief and his accomplice
Cracking their bones in a door
How well he understood impertinence
How swiftly he forestalled apology with
The lightning pleasures of revenge

He has gone away today leaving the curtains drawn
Some affidavit from a distant place
Represents him as an executioner

The gale roars through my greasy jackets
As if my ribs were open railings of wet iron
No character within
No substance of identity

Tear my poor conflicts away
Blow my arguments with the salt spray
Over the roofs of the churches

All I believed is false
Yes
And what has rushed in is false also
Tomorrow will reveal

A youth
Of sufficient cleanliness
Kneels at the feet of the female tramp
Such an idealist
Her odour loses all offence

Alas
She
Has
Acquired
So
Little
From
Destitution

I know I heard her laugh

Stop investigating for God's
Do you think truth prefers the gutter
Stop flattering yourself you are her equal
Stop smoothing the raw disorders
With your inquisitive sleeve

You have a monarch's condescension
Wrapped in slang
Even your crouching is sly
The arrogant bid of impossible closure

And there are gaols floating like mirages
Behind your charitable eye

Even the dogs are staggering in the gale
Their legs are pins of insecurity
And the pebbles stirred from sloth
Are ringing like mirrors

HELLO YOU MATES OF WRATH
HOW YOUR ANGER KEEPS YOU LISSOME
YOU ARE SPRING HEELED WITH THE
ALCOHOL
       OF
         NEVER
            GIVING
                YOUR
                    ASSENT

I could die now
So near to your house
And the stars could lick me off the kerb

OH THIS MONOTONOUS HOSTILITY WHAT
COULD BE WORSE ONLY MONOTONOUS LOVE

Old woman your song makes you cry
With the sound of your disintegration
I also could cry
But I prefer to deride your
Face of an orange burst by wheels

Permit me to pass
I am not like you admittedly
In all things we are opposites
No possibility of reconciliation
Can exist
All smiles are fakes
All gestures false
If we derived from planets of
Milennial hostility
Our distinction could not yell
It louder
Still
Permit me to pass for civility's sake

I have so many sick relatives
But I insist on smiling my art
Even the criminals look ill
But still I call my art
As a man whistles his lingering mongrel